TOPIARY

Garden Craftsmanship in Yew and Box

TOPIARY

Garden Craftsmanship in Yew and Box

Nathaniel Lloyd

Preface by
Christopher Lloyd

GARDEN ART PRESS

Frontispiece: HIGHAM, SUSSEX. *Strongly battlemented yews and low box hedges contain the roses and restrain the woodland beyond the lawn.*

Title page: GREAT DIXTER, SUSSEX. *Pyramids of yew support stylised topiary birds below the soaring chimneys of the ancient house.*

Front cover: GREAT DIXTER, SUSSEX.

Back cover: GREAT DIXTER, SUSSEX.

Printed in England on Consort Royal Satin paper from Donside Mills, Aberdeen, Scotland
by the Antique Collectors' Club, Woodbridge, Suffolk IP12 1DS, UK

CONTENTS

GREAT DIXTER, SUSSEX. *The great stepped arch, through which the path leads to the topiary bird garden.*

GREAT DIXTER. SUSSEX. *Formal box creations flank the timbered porch, emphasizing the entrance.*

GREAT DIXTER, SUSSEX. *Formal yews dominate a feathery Cotinus coggygria on the lower lawn.*

BRICKWALL HOUSE, SUSSEX. *Shaped yews and box edging lead to the arch beyond flower borders.*

NOTE FROM THE
PUBLISHER

The publisher wishes to thank the management of Great Dixter for allowing original photographic prints from the original book to be reproduced in this new edition.

BRICKWALL HOUSE, SUSSEX. *Snow sharpens the profiles of the topiary specimens and chess frames leading to the distant house.*

PREFACE

The planting and cultivation of yew has long been an important element in garden design, but there is no adequate, reliable treatise dealing with these matters, and the art of topiary is jealously guarded by the professional grower. The following pages set forth in detail methods which have proved satisfactory in practice in respect of hedges, arches and clipped specimens in yew and box.

NATHANIEL LLOYD.

GREAT DIXTER,
NORTHIAM.

PITMEDDEN, GRAMPIAN. *Box scrolls in a precision parterre emphasized by solid geometry and edging.*

HOLME PIERREPONT HALL, NOTTINGHAMSHIRE. *A Victorian parterre, edged in box, with multicoloured floral planting typical of the period.*

PITMEDDEN, GRAMPIAN. *Triangular geometry in box hedging contains bedding plants in formal parterres.*

Plate 1. *Vista through yew archway.*
Formed of 4 ft. plants put in twelve years earlier.

To
My Friends,

Amateur topiarists and professional gardeners,
whose keen interest and invaluable assistance
have developed these possibilities in Yew and
Box, this little book is dedicated

Plate 2. GREAT DIXTER, SUSSEX. *Steps and hedges provide a strong structure,
beyond which a yew 'chocolate pot' stands sentinel before the building.*

GREAT DIXTER, SUSSEX. *Beyond this colourful herbaceous border yew hedges and smooth sculptural shapes dominate the upper vistas.*

PREFACE–1995 EDITION

Seventy years after its first publication, my father's book is in print again. That is great news. It shows two things: that the interest in topiary and in yew and box hedging in general is still alive; and that the book has stood up to the test of time. New examples have been added to the photographs in this edition; the text remains the same.

This is a practical work, based on my father's own experience in establishing yew and box topiary and hedging at Dixter, after my parents moved into their home in 1912. And there are many examples from elsewhere. Nathaniel Lloyd was taking his own photographs all over the country, in preparation for the two great publications which followed: *A History of English Brickwork* and *A History of the English House.*

He loved precision; hence his emphasis on exact lines and levels and precisely flat surfaces. Yews, however, are nearly always raised from seed. Each seedling being genetically different, there are inevitably differences in form, colour and vigour between the units in any given stretch of hedge. Therefore the sternness of battlemented bastions tends, in time, to give evidence of unintended swellings and obesity in unlooked-for directions.

I find this kind of divergence hilarious. Solemnity is dissipated in a gale of laughter. And topiary itself is a kind of fun, never intended to be taken too seriously, however cleverly executed. Those who sneer at it as a childish exercise are lacking in a sense of humour. Topiary goes through phases of being unfashionable, but it always bounces back.

A COUNTRY GARDEN, SUSSEX. *Parallel yew hedges, with entrances emphasized by domed finials, divide farmland from garden with dark green rigidity.*

A good deal of topiary has vanished in my lifetime, much of it of cottage garden status. Cottagers used to be static over generations, which is what suits the love and care of topiary. People are far more mobile, now, and they lack the stability to train their topiary pieces and to maintain them over the years. More of this art is now retained on large properties that are open to the public.

But hedging and topiary in yew and box is open to every gardener and these small-leaved materials are ideal for the purpose. Just aim for broad effect and don't try to be too elaborate or clever. Satisfactions that are spread over the years are those that last.

CHRISTOPHER LLOYD

THE GARDEN

The word "garden," whether traced to French, Dutch or German origins, signifies an enclosure: indeed it is within everyone's knowledge that the actual sense of being in a garden is not experienced (whatever the cultivation) except when there is also a feeling of enclosure. Without such enclosure, as may happen when a new garden is laid out upon an open site (before walls are built or hedges have grown up), the feelings of protection, of peacefulness and of repose are altogether lacking.

It is not surprising, therefore, that the garden maker strives to secure something more than an open fence to keep out cattle. Perhaps there is no more desirable form of enclosure than an old stone or brick wall the joints of which may be richly studded with wall-loving plants, but a new wall needs more than one generation to mature to such a state. Next, for screen and background to borders, come hedges, for which a host of bush and tree plants, suitable and unsuitable, have been employed. Deciduous bushes, such as whitethorn or quick, though excellent as screens and on account of their rapidity of growth, are not comparable as backgrounds with evergreens. Of these the common yew, *Taxus baccata*, is superior to all others. That yew is slow of growth is one of those popular fallacies the origin of which is difficult to imagine, for it is actually one of the quickest growing of all hedge plants, and no other so well responds to suitable treatment. The small leaves or needles do not look unsightly when cut as do those of big-leafed plants like laurel, and if properly clipped the plants do not become lean and stalky near the ground like privet,

GREAT DIXTER, SUSSEX. *Variations on formalized bird shapes perch on the pyramidical yews leading to the stepped arch.*

thuya and arbor vitae. Yew also possesses the advantage of readily being trimmed to any shapes desired. This property (shared by the slower-growing box) has long been appreciated by gardeners.

The importance of the formal garden as a setting to the house is too well established to require vindication here, and yew hedges form a suitable link between the purely architectural lay-out which is essential in the immediate vicinity of the house, and such wild and more unsophisticated treatment as may be in keeping at a little distance. Formal gardening, introduced here in the first half of the sixteenth century, became general before the end of

Hedge framework, with decorative fantasies, used to shape country hedges, from Markham's The Country Farm, *published in the early 17th century.*

HAMPTON COURT, MIDDLESEX. *The sunken garden, with box peacocks and floral planting round the formal terracing.*

Elizabeth's reign. It was based upon the Italian gardens of the Renaissance but these had their prototypes in Roman gardens, and, in the first century, Pliny writes of box cut into shapes of animals. Yew was planted at Hampton Court by Henry VIII; and Bacon speaks of topiary work executed in juniper, box and yew. At the present time the sound revival of garden planning upon architectural lines has emphasized the importance of yew for hedges, even more than for topiary work. Many failures, however, occur through lack of knowledge on the part of gardeners and other persons concerned with planting and maintenance.

HOLE PARK, SUSSEX. *Monumentally rectangular pillars, capped by half-spherical domes, stand like gate-columns at the entrances to these yew hedge walls.*

A COUNTRY GARDEN, SUSSEX. *By scooping out this hedge at its junction with another hedge set at right angles, and embellishing the lower level with a flattened ball finial, the topiarist has used decorative flair to create architectural interest.*

HEDGES

With a view to showing the rapidity of the growth of yew, when suitably treated, records have been kept of eight hedges, noting the sizes of the plants when put in, the treatment of ground, and manner of planting and describing the different kinds of soils. By this means a clear idea can be had of the possibilities of yew and the best means of obtaining matured hedges in a short time.

HIGHAM, SUSSEX. *The castle-wall impression given by these battlemented yew hedges serves to emphasize the division of ordered lawns and gardens from the naturalism of surrounding trees and shrubs.*

SUDELEY CASTLE, GLOUCESTERSHIRE. *A celebrated hedge, massive and chamfered, pierced by arched alcoves to lighten the solidity and perhaps provide for statuary.*

CRATHES CASTLE, ABERDEENSHIRE. *An upper window view of the passage between enormous yew hedges flanked, at the entrance, by specimens formed into truncated cones.*

PORT LYMPNE, KENT. *Wide, flattened yew hedges, scooped and squared, surround a colourful garden.*

GREAT DIXTER, SUSSEX. *The curving, low box hedging draws the eye towards an opening in the powerful yew walls, behind which a great domed tree of the same species and the timbered house are sheltered.*

Plate 3. HIGHAM: hedge round lawn borders as planted.
The plants are somewhat scanty and not well furnished, but the ground was well prepared. Plants three feet high.

Results of Planting Yew Hedges of Various Sizes in Different Soils

Nos.	Size when planted	Size in 12 years as clipped		
		Height	Base width	Top width
T.L.1.	6 x 2-ft. pillars sold as hedge plants	8½	4½	1¾ ft.
R.G.2.	4½ x 1¾ ft. pillars	7	4	2½ ft.
O.G.3.	3-ft. pyramids, 2-ft at base	2ft. 7½	4½	1½ ft.
H.G.4.	3-ft. pillars, about 1¼ ft. at base	6	5	1¼ ft.
H.G.5.	Do.	7	5	1½ ft.
H.G.6.	Do.	8	5½	2 ft.
O.7.	Nursery plants 1 ft. high	In nine years: 6	3½	1¾ ft.
H.	3-ft. pyramids, scanty foliage	In four years, as clipped: 4	3	1 ft.

Plate 4. HIGHAM: *The hedge shown in Plate 3 four years later.*

Situation and Treatment

Ground dug 4 ft. wide and 2½ ft. deep, 2-in. land drain at bottom of trench, covered brick rubble. Then 9in. soil, with dung. On this 6in. soil, and filled up with soil and a little well-rotted dung in which plants set. Clay soil. Turf both sides. A very wet position.

Treatment as last. Heavy loam. Turf one side: on other side (to prevent roots reaching rose beds) a barrier of galvanized iron 2½ ft. wide bedded in the ground on its edge was interposed.

On old hedge bank, double dug 2 ft. deep; dung dug into bottom spit; old dung in top spit. Border 3 ft. away both sides. Medium loam.

Planted broadside to wind. Rough grass one side, kitchen garden other side, dug 2½ ft. No. 1A. Sandy loam.

End on to wind. Rough grass one side, kitchen garden the other side. Sandy loam.

End on to wind. Garden both sides. Sandy loam.

On old hedge bank; ditch both sides, overshadowed by trees and high hedge 8ft. to S.E. Dug, etc., as O.G.3. Medium loam.

Well dug and manured herbaceous border; sandy loam, overlying sandstone rock.

GODINTON PARK, KENT. *The profile cut at the top of the formal yew hedging echoes the shape of the gables of the house.*

HIGHAM, SUSSEX. *The shaping of these hedges enlivens what might have been a severe boundary to the garden. The pattern of light and shade created by domes and channels cut into the upper structure adds excitement to the solidity of the composition.*

It should be noted that the dimensions after several years are much less than if the clipping each season had not been very drastic: the object being to obtain close, compact growth rather than large size.

These tabulated records show quickest and most economical results with the 3-ft. pyramids, and this advantage is still more marked in view of the severe losses experienced with the 4½-ft. and 6-ft. plants, the mortality of which was from 30 per cent to 50 per cent. Moreover, these large plants, not being fully furnished down to the ground,

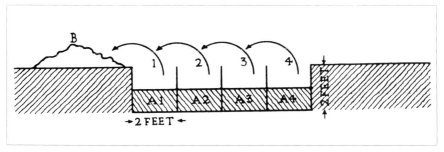

DOUBLE DIGGING.
Lower spit, A1, A2, etc., forked up with dung. The top spit from No1 is thrown out at B until wanted to fill up at the other end of trench.

were very thin and scanty looking for several years; whereas the 3-ft. pyramids, which were bushy near the ground when planted, formed a solid hedge in less than four years, and with few losses. The 3-ft. pillars sold as plants for making hedges were not bushy near the ground, and took many years to fill out low down; whereas plants which started thin at the top soon grew together into good hedges. It may be laid down as an axiom that it takes two to three times as long to grow a good base to a plant as to fill in at the top. All plants grow quickly if the ground is well and deeply dug, as illustrated, but thorough drainage is essential in heavy soils. Without this, water lies in the dug ground and the roots stand in water all winter. The consequence is that the foliage turns coppery, and, if the waterlogged condition continues, the needles turn a pale colour and the plant dies. Where it was necessary to keep the yew roots out of a rose border, as in R.G.2, by interposing a vertical barrier of sheet galvanized iron, the ground on the other side of the hedge was dug and cultivated 4 ft. out. Roots were not allowed to come within 6 ins. of the dung at the bottom of the trenches, and only short, well-rotted manure was mixed with the soil in which the yews were planted. The roots were planted rather high (about 4 ins. up) that water might drain from their stems, and trodden in very firmly. It was found that spring was a better time to plant than autumn, when the looser soil tended to become waterlogged. In an exposed situation,

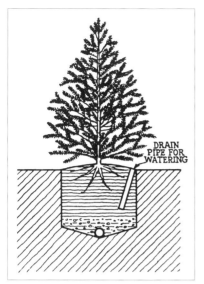

(above left). Section through drained trench. Tree planted high.
(above right). Plate 5. PILLARS SOLD AS HEDGE PLANTS. *Those broadside to the wind are screened with canvas. For growth, see table, p. 24. No H.G.4.*

April was found a good time to plant, when the gales, which strained the roots, had abated. Where a hedge was planted broadside to the south, it was sheltered for a year by canvas screens 3½ft. high, Plate 5, to protect from the pressure of wind. In some years, long droughts, with bright sun and drying winds, were experienced in early summer. The labour of frequent watering was reduced by setting one 2-in. land drain on end in the ground between each plant, one end being just on the surface (this was covered with a piece of tile to reduce evaporation) and water poured down it to the roots of the plants. This served a double purpose by substituting weekly for daily watering and by drawing roots downwards into wet ground instead of upwards to be scorched by sun, after water poured on the surface had evaporated. In exceptional seasons an occasional drenching of foliage in the evening was also very helpful to the larger plants.[1] Yews should not be clipped until at least one year after planting: actually not before the September

1. By the same method yews could be maintained in countries where summers are fiercely hot or droughty

(above) GREAT DIXTER, SUSSEX. *The strength of this opening comes from the use of stone steps, yew bastions and solid, if asymmetric, hedge battlements to complement the dominant house and chimneys.*

(opposite above) KNIGHTSHAYES, DEVON. *Like medieval castle walls, these yew hedges enclose hidden lawns and ponds accessible only via narrow arched entrances cut through the thick, tightly-clipped growth.*

(opposite below) GREAT DIXTER, SUSSEX. *A stepped arch enlivens the access through this yew hedge dividing a formal garden from the spaces beyond.*

Plate 6. THE BEST CLASS OF PLANT FOR HEDGES
Pyramids, well furnished down to the ground, which quickly grow together at the top. Compare with Plate 7, taken twelve years later from the same spot.

twelvemonth after planting. The roots will then have had time to make fresh growth and so to consolidate as to be firmly established. It must be remembered that cutting away the top shoot or leader always throws a plant back. The heights of trees will vary a little, no matter how even a lot may have been sent out by the nurseryman, and effort should be made at first clipping to bring these to an average height. Cutting the tops out of the taller plants will cause them to fill out sideways whilst the shorter ones are growing up to them, and so to fill up the intervals between the plants. The second clipping, a year later, should produce a fairly even, level and compact hedge.

The foregoing remarks apply particularly to plants several feet in height, such as are put in to get a good hedge in the shortest time. It will be seen, however, that the most economical and satisfactory results in other respects were obtained with nursery plants only 1 ft. high. These cost one-twelfth what the 3-ft. plants did; practically none were lost, and they required little attention after planting. Although

Plate 7. A NARROW ARCHWAY
A narrow archway (four feet across) formed by tying twigs together and clipping to shape by eye alone.

they caught up the 3-ft. plants in about nine years, they did not make so good a hedge after only three or four years' growth. At the other extreme were the 6-ft. plants, which were very costly, and difficult to keep alive in an unfavourable season; notwithstanding their height they made but a thin, poor hedge for several years. Whatever sized plants may be chosen, it is well to obtain a sample plant from the supplier who quotes, and it should be

(above left) SISSINGHURST, KENT. *Hedging used to create an alcove for statuary.*
(above right) CHATSWORTH, DERBYSHIRE. *Bottle-shaped yews add emphasis to the vista contained by hedges.*

stipulated that the sample shall represent the minimum size which will be sent in execution of order. The usual practice of sending an average sample may result in disappointment when the bulk comes forward. In inviting tenders from nurserymen, regard should be paid to the class of soil in which the plants have been grown. To bring plants from poor or clayey soil to put them in rich well-drained loam will result satisfactorily; but to take them from rich soil and plant in that which is light and hungry, or to set them in stiff waterlogged clay, will result in many losses, slow growth and poor hedges. If very large plants (5 to 6 ft. high) are contemplated, it is well to ascertain that they have been moved every few years, and that the last move took place not more than three years previously. Plants which have been moved from time to time will have many compact, fibrous roots; whereas trees which have not been disturbed for many years will probably have large, coarse, tap roots, which must necessarily be severed in the operation of lifting and make the plant's survival after replanting an exceedingly doubtful prospect.

These well-shaped young yews will eventually grow to form a dense hedge around this garden.

When plants arrive from the nurseryman, the roots should be examined, and if dry they should be soaked in water for twelve hours or longer before laying into trenches pending planting. The sooner they are planted, however, the better their chances of survival. The distance plants should be set apart will depend upon their size and upon how urgently a compact hedge is required. If possible, 2½ to 3 ft. between stems should be allowed, but small plants or those having scanty foliage may be set closer. When hedges are well grown they may suffer severe injury if a heavy fall of snow lies on them, and snow, therefore, should not be allowed to accumulate.

After yews are established, the ground for at least 2 ft. round them should be well hoed or forked up three or four times a year, and once a year well dressed with such manure as basic slag, sprinkled on the newly worked soil and allowed to wash in. A good month in which to do this is March.

CLIPPING

If yews are clipped late in August or during September, the work will be completed before frosts are severe, and, as the growth will then have been made for the season, hedges and topiary work will remain sharp and tidy until fresh growth is made the following summer: actually for eight or nine months. In hedge-clipping there is only one essential to be observed, which is to have the greatest thickness at ground level and gradually to reduce this all the way up. The sloping face thus produced is what a mason would call the "batter" of a wall; but whereas a batter of 1 in. to each foot rise is sufficient for a garden wall, yew hedges should have from 2 to 4 ins. batter to each foot of height. Batter has two merits: one that it makes the hedge look substantial, the other that it allows the lower boughs of the plant to receive sun and air, which stimulates their growth. On the other hand, should this lower foliage be recessed and overhung by that above it, the result will be weak growth, resulting eventually in exposure of the stems and spoiling of the hedge. Where this has occurred in old hedges, the only course to pursue is to cut all branches and foliage back severely, even as far as the main stems of the plants, and thus to encourage fresh growth to break, which in a few years will form a good battered face to the hedge. This was the course adopted some years ago to the high hedge at the foot of the sunk garden at Penshurst Place, Plate 8, which is now greatly improved and would be better still if cut with a batter. The practice in this garden is to aim at a vertical face to hedges, with the result that the foliage of the upper branches thrives more vigorously than that below, and thus

Plate 8. PENSHURST PLACE, KENT. *Hedge around rose garden.*

Tools used for hedge clipping and topiary work.

A yew hedge which has been severely cut back. It will grow again, with dense coverage forming on the bare branches.

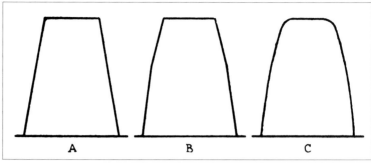

VARIOUS BATTERS FOR HEDGES

A. A uniform batter of 2 ins. to the foot, cut flat at top, with sharp angles.
B. A batter of 1½ins. to the foot for the first 3 ft., and 3 ins. to the foot for the next
  2 ft., cut flat at top, with sharp angles.
C. A batter of 1½ins. to the foot for the first 3 ft., and of 3 ins. to the foot for the
  next 2 ft.; the top is cut flat, but the angles are rounded.

tends slightly to overhang, so destroying just that vertical effect it is desired to produce. It is not necessary that the amount of batter should the the same all the way up. The hedge round the Rose Garden at Dixter, Plate 9, has a batter of 3 ins. to the foot; but the buttresses have a batter of 1½ ins. to the foot for the first 3 ft. and of 3 ins. to the foot for the next 2 ft. The sketches A, B, C show sections of three methods of battering.

A is a good treatment for hedges such as those at Penshurst (Plate 8) which are to have domes or semicircular finials rising from the flat tops.

B produces a more substantial effect, and is particularly suitable when a walled appearance is desired as for the Rose Garden at Dixter, Plate 9.

C is the most substantial and matured-looking treatment of all and is particularly suited to homely, old-fashioned garden design, as distinguished from more formal and classic layouts. The illustrations of hedges nearest this section are those of the hedge beyond the pool at Brickwall, Plate 11, and the hedge in the cottage garden at Frant, Plate 20. The batters mentioned are not the only ones that may be employed: indeed, there is room for considerable exercise of judgment in varying the batters of hedges in different

Plate 9. GREAT DIXTER, SUSSEX. *Yew hedge round rose garden, with piers and buttresses. All cut with a batter to produce severe, massive wall effect. This hedge, designed by Sir Edwin Lutyens, is the only hedge with a flat top in the garden.*

Plate 10. INSTRUMENT FOR DETERMININING BATTER, AND TO CHECK ACCURACY OF CLIPPING. *The batter of this hedge, No. H.G.6. p.24, is four inches to each foot of height. The cross batten at the top is marked with lines, each of which represents an inch batter to a foot in height. A pin passing through a hole in the guide, to holes in the cross-piece, keeps this to the batter required.*

Plate 11. TANK GARDEN AT BRICKWALL
Extreme simplicity with consequent reposeful feeling is the characteristic of these hedges and conical piers.

situations ; batter exceeding 4 ins. to the foot may be given and will encourage thick growth.

The introduction of piers, buttresses and simple finials at well-considered intervals greatly enhances the importance of yew hedges, but these should be plain and simple in form, or the air of repose and dignity which the garden should possess will suffer. Fanciful forms of birds, etc., on hedges are better suited to the cottage garden and to specimen trees of the topiary garden proper, of which mention will be made later.

As will be seen in the illustrations, yew hedges owe much of their charm to the accuracy with which they have been trimmed and to the care taken to keep their tops perfectly level. One has only to compare such a hedge with a quick-thorn hedge as trimmed by farm labourers. Though wide at the top, it is thin at the bottom, with many gaps, and its

PITMEDDEN, GRAMPIAN. *Yew buttresses, curved downwards to accommodate ball finials.*

CHATSWORTH, DERBYSHIRE. *Simple buttresses add structure and rhythm to the boundary wall.*

Magnificently battered hedges with buttresses adding emphasis and strength of design at regular intervals.

A country hedge with clipped holly trees spaced at regular intervals to add decorative emphasis to this form of boundary.

levels wander up and down with the contours of the ground. As a matter of fact this is all quite unnecessary, and is the result of carelessness and ignorance. Such thorn hedges have been taken in hand and had applied to them the treatment given to yew hedges, with the result that (following drastic cutting in the first year) in a few years they were narrow at the top, wide near the ground, evenly covered with verdure and not only pleasing to see, but efficient as fences and no longer requiring repairs and expenditure for stakes and labour.

When the height has been determined to which a yew hedge is to be cut that season (if desired, the height may be

Plate 12. *The level of the top of the hedge is marked by string and is now ready for clipping.*

(above left) Plate 13. *Line to guide the extent of cutting back new growth.*
(above right) Plate 14. *If cutting a high hedge it is helpful to have someone steady the ladder.*

Plate 15. *Testing level of old hedge top with short batten and spirit level.*

increased according to the growth made each year), a strong stake of, say, 2 ins. diameter should be driven into the ground through the branches near to the proposed top of batter. This stake should have its top the exact height to which the hedge is to be trimmed. Five or six feet along the hedge another stake is to be driven into the ground in a similar position, until its top is on the same level as the first stake. This level is determined by means of a straight-edged board of sufficient length to bridge the interval and rest on the tops of the stakes (any carpenter will plane a "deal" for the purpose); on the upper ledge of this board the spirit-level is laid, Plates 15 and 16. The stakes having been tested and found level, a string is stretched between them, resting on their tops and continued to another stake as far along the hedge as required. If this cannot be strained sufficiently to prevent sagging, it must be supported by slight intermediate stakes, but, even where this is done, the level must be tested from time to time to ensure its having been preserved, as it is liable to be disturbed during cutting and also by the intervention of twigs of yew with which the string will be in contact. When the hedge has a very wide top, it will be necessary to find and mark the level (as described with

Plate 16. *The guiding string is still in position but the hedge has been cut.*

stakes and string) on *both* sides. Once a hedge has been properly levelled, the annual cutting can be done by eye assisted by a short piece of batten and a spirit-level, Plate 17) except for long levels, for which a guide string is

Plate 17. *Testing level of old hedge top with short batten and spirit level.*

Well-cut pyramidical yews add height to this horizontally-designed garden.

Plate 18. BATEMAN'S.
The use of yew to stop a view and as a background and shelter for a garden seat.

HEVER CASTLE, KENT. *Trimming topiary.*

desirable. Of course the levelling stakes are removed after cutting, but the two should not be drawn up until the whole length of hedge has been cut, for it is from them that all extensions of level are projected.

Festina lente should be the motto of the topiarist. It is better to cut away less than is anticipated will be necessary, and to go over the area a second time, than to risk cutting too much and have to wait several seasons' growth to make good the error. Cones are easier to clip than pyramids: indeed all circular work is easier than flat surfaces, and it is well to practise in circular work first until a certain degree of proficiency with shears has been attained, remembering that the whole charm of such work depends upon the precision with which it is done.

TOPIARY SPECIMEN TREES

The practice of cutting trees into shapes of birds and animals, practised by the Romans and revived in the Middle Ages, was introduced into England with other architectural adjuncts. Like every art, it may be abused, but, treated with restraint, such clipped trees introduced singly, in pairs or in groups, provide a certain atmosphere in a garden which is not to be obtained by any other means. The fantastic shapes and figures at Earlshall, Plate 19, soften the severity of their architectural background, to which they

Plate 19. TOPIARY GARDEN AT EARLSHALL
These trees were moved as six foot cones twenty years earlier.

RENNES, FRANCE. *The proportion of these bird-topped topiaries would have been improved by allowing a wider base diameter to the supporting cones. As it is, there is a slightly top-heavy look to the creations.*

Plate 20. YEW TREE COTTAGES, FRANT
A good example of yew hedge and finials as treated by cottagers. Too much of such treatment would be tiresome.

afford a pleasing contrast, and the plump, odd shapes on the cottage-garden hedge at Frant, Plate 20, are exactly suited to a small garden, and worthy of better buildings behind them. In specimen trees, as in yew hedges, there is virtue in great bulk: hence the attenuated topiary plants grown in Holland and imported here require many years before they confer the right quality upon the gardens in which they are placed. Large trees of this kind are exceedingly costly, and better effects can be obtained by purchasing large, bushy, cone-shaped trees in England and starting to trim them into shape when established after removal. If such trees are planted in ground prepared as described for hedges, well supported for such time as is

ATHELHAMPTON, DORSET. *A pair of topiary figures intended eventually to be shaped as king and queen figures, but with the heads not yet formed.*

MOUNT EPHRAIM, KENT. *Specimen yews demonstrating formal and layered shapes.*

BRICKWALL, SUSSEX. *The metal frames for the topiary chess garden set out in front of the existing shaped yews.*

Plate 21. *Circle of simple yew cones at Brickwall.*

necessary (this will vary according to the sheltered or exposed nature of the site) by stakes concealed within their foliage, they will soon present a better appearance than the meagre imported trees and in very few years surpass these in every respect. Such shapes as the cone with button top,

BRICKWALL, SUSSEX. *The yews lining the avenue have been allowed to wander from the original formal pyramid shaping shown in the illustration below.*

Plate 22. AVENUE OF TETRAHEDRONS AT BRICKWALL.
Planted about two hundred years ago.

Plate 23, can be formed from good plants of suitable size three years after moving. The cones at Brickwall, Plate 21, are exceedingly effective in groups. They are of great age, but similar sizes might be obtained with good 6-ft. trees in twelve years, if properly planted and tended. After only

This roughly-shaped yew tree could be trimmed to produce a cone with a button finial, as shown in Plate 23.

Plate 23. *Cone with button finial.*

three years they would look compact and shapely. The trees on each side of the pathway at Brickwall, Plate 22, are over two hundred years old, but they also could be produced in a tenth part of that time. They are not pyramids but tetrahedrons, being triangular in plan. Natural developments of the cone and button, Plate 23, are the coffee-pots, Plate 24, while the teapot at Sedlescombe, Plate 25, and the sitting bird, Plate 26, from the same village belong to this class of treatment: indeed no sooner is a design like the cone and button completed than it suggests its own development. Peacocks and other birds with wide-spread tails are favourite subjects because they are extremely effective (the more wooden looking, the better they are) and are easy to form. It is only necessary to choose a plant suitable for the purpose in view.

Plate 24. *Yew coffee-pots with yew piers beyond. There is room for greater variety of shapes in specimen yews, provided these are simple and substantial.*

Plate 25. *Teapot formed out of bunch of twigs by cottager.*

Plate 26. *A sitting bird.*

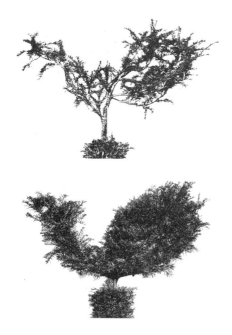

(above) GREAT DIXTER, SUSSEX. *A fully grown peacock.*
Plate 27a & b. FORMING A PEACOCK
(above left) A. First stage: training to shape with strong fencing wire.
(left) B. Second stage: after two years.

(above left) Plate 28. FORMING A PEACOCK
Another method: by tying together several stems and using the longest for head and tail. Other birds in process of shaping may be seen in the background.

(above right) Plate 29. FORMING A PEACOCK
The same tree one year later.

GREAT DIXTER, SUSSEX. *Truncated cones of solid appearance support bird shapes clustered companionably together with the house seen beyond.*

If the peacock is to stand upon one stem, a tree must be chosen which has one main stem, with two twigs branching at the point where the bird is to rest. These are bent, the smaller to the angle of the proposed bird's neck, the larger into a loop and both are secured in position by stout fencing wire. Other twigs and branches which can be utilized to form tail or body are tied into position and superfluous growths cut away, as in the illustration, Plate 27a. The development of such a bird is shown in illustration, Plate 27b. If it is not essential that the bird should stand on a single stem, the body may be formed by tying twigs together and leaving longer stems from which to grow head and tail, as in Plates 28 and 29. By this means large objects may be modelled in a short time, and this is how most of the cottage subjects illustrated have been started: indeed this treatment is possibly that best suited to a growing material.

A crown is formed by bending over and downwards four twigs, which grow symmetrically from the stem: their points

Elevation of crown with nearest twig cut away

Plan of crown from above

Formation of terminal ring on stout wire

NYMANS, SUSSEX. *Cylindrical yew bases provide visually solid support to the complex crown topiaries set round a pond.*

being tied with tarred string to the stem below. As the natural habit of twigs and branches is to grow upward, a better curve is obtained by tying down and obviates the necessity for using wire to form the curves. When, however, a ring is to be formed at the top of a tree, stout wire must be secured to the stem just below two branching twigs, and turned in a circle round which the twigs may be trained for

A typical box spiral in a pot, put out for sale at a garden centre.

LEVENS HALL, CUMBRIA. A view of the celebrated garden with the gables of the house capping a high circle of yew.

the ring. Spirals may be formed by cutting back the foliage of a tree which has one central stem, or by choosing a young yew plant sufficiently pliable to train round a stout stake, driven into the ground *before* the yew is planted against it. Such a stem will grow upwards very quickly, and side growths should be cut away so as to preserve the gradually tapering and compactly grown spiral. A *chestnut* stake 3 ins. in diameter which has been barked and had the point creosoted up to a foot above ground will last for many years until the stem of the yew is well set in the required twist. There is no limit to the diameter of the stake used. If a very open spiral is required several stakes may be grouped in the centre.

It must be remembered that once a start is made to form a finial, the height of the tree is then approximately determined, consequently

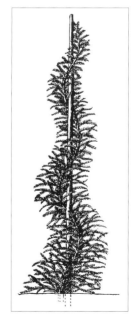

Method of forming spiral round stake, beginning with 1 year old plant

COTTAGE TOPIARY, CUMBRIA. *An arch and formal, layered fantasies at the entrance gate to a cottage garden.*

the formation of finials cannot be begun until the tree has attained the full height of base required. Forming birds and other shapes is so easily done that any intelligent person can undertake them. It is the first step that intimidates the beginner, but even the simplest beginning will suggest its own development so obviously that it becomes difficult to

RODMARTEN, GLOUCESTERSHIRE. *Topiary specimens of well-formed proportions.*

Plate 30. LEAF MOOR COTTAGES, FRANT. *The fussy finials over the great arch at the gate are out of keeping with its dignity and mass.*

LADEW GARDENS, USA. *A swan in course of formation, with guiding framework shown in not yet filled condition.*

realize there was ever any problem. Simple, substantial-looking shapes are best. Fussy, finical forms are especially to be avoided. The massive dignified effect of the gateway arch of Leaf Moor Cottages, Plate 30, is ruined by the trivial devices by which it is surmounted. These may be compared with the well-chosen shapes on the hedge at Yew Tree Cottages, Plate 20.

Wire guides and string ties should be watched to prevent constriction of stems by delay in re-tying, or the plant will deteriorate rapidly.

HEVER CASTLE, KENT. *An excellent example of a spiral, topped by a bird, mounted on a strong-looking cylindrical base.*

MOVING LARGE TREES

It sometimes happens that old, naturally-grown yew trees, Plate 31, are near a house or so placed in a garden that they would be better clipped to shape than if left in their natural state. To effect this change, the branches must be cut back as shown in illustration, Plate 32, when the tree will throw out a multitude of fresh shoots and, in a few years, may be cut to any suitable form that is desired. Plates 33, 34, and 35 show intermediate stages. Umbrella-shaped trees, as

Plate 31. *The tree in top left corner is that illustrated in Plates 32-35.*

Plate 32. TOPIARY TREATMENT OF A NATURAL GROWN YEW TREE.
Fresh growth two years after cutting back to the stem at the top, and lower branches back to three feet long.

Plate 33. TOPIARY TREATMENT OF A NATURAL GROWN YEW TREE.
New growth after six years.

Plate 34. TOPIARY TREATMENT OF A NATURAL GROWN YEW TREE.
New growth after nine years; shaping begun.

Plate 35. TOPIARY TREATMENT OF A NATURAL GROWN YEW TREE.
The same tree from another point of view, after nine and a half years, showing development of form.

Plate 32.

Plate 33.

Plate 34.

Plate 35.

COTTAGE TOPIARY, SUSSEX. *A yew 'mushroom' or 'umbrella' shape which ensures that even light distribution and growth are obtained as far as possible.*

THE NATIONAL PINETUM, BEDGEBURY, SUSSEX. *Removal of a tree ready for transplanting. Photo credit: Colin Morgan, Curator, National Pinetum, Bedgebury.*

those at Hampton Court, can be formed in this way and most naturally-grown, old trees lend themselves to this shape.

Large trees may be moved successfully, but the degree of such success will depend much upon how large a ball of earth is retained round the roots and upon how short a time elapses before replanting. Trees which with their ball of earth weigh up to 8 cwt., may be raised and moved by half a dozen men. The ball of roots and earth should be about 4 ft. across and 2½ft. deep; by the time it is moved the latter measurement will have been reduced to 2 ft. by crumbling away of earth. The soil must be damp throughout. If dry, it will not hold together; if too wet, it will be greasy and sticky, so as almost to be impossible to work. All roots for 2 ft. around the tree and more than 2½ft. under the surface of the ground should be cut away, including any tap root. The ground should be opened for several feet round, as necessitated by the situation, so that men engaged may work conveniently. Any long branches should be raised and tied up close to the trunk. A piece of strong canvas, such as is used by furniture removers, 15 ft. square, is inserted under the ball. This is done by pulling the tree over on its side, folding and pushing the canvas as far under as possible (as a nurse puts a sheet under a patient who cannot leave bed) and then rocking the tree in the opposite direction, which will enable the canvas to be drawn still further under. This process is repeated (if necessary) until the ball of earth and roots stands in the middle of the canvas. The canvas is then drawn up to the trunk and tied securely so that the four corners form four large ears, which will afford good handles of which the men may take hold. The tree is then rocked on one side and earth thrown under and rammed tightly. On this rammed earth the tree is rocked to the other side, further earth thrown in where it was lying and rammed hard. The process is repeated until the canvas ball has been raised nearly to the original ground level, when it can be rocked, pushed and lifted on to planks, along which it can be pushed with levers and pulled by the canvas ears. At the end of the planks or under them, as may be most convenient, a Samson trolley may be brought and the ball slid or dropped on to this, Plate 36. Then it can be wheeled on planks used as rails to its new position, where it may be slid into the hole prepared for it and, by rocking from side to side, the canvas be folded and withdrawn in the same way as it was got under. It will be found that six or seven men are as many as can work together round the ball, which limits the size of

Plate 36. MOVING A YEW TREE.
Roots of large tree enclosed in canvas, tied with handles for lifting. Weight of tree and earth round roots about four hundredweight.

tree and ball which can be handled without special appliances. The new site for the tree should be drained and prepared as described for hedges. The tree should be firmly staked and secured for many years after removal, until it has

CHANNEL TUNNEL, KENT. *Semi-mature trees being unloaded by crane before planting at the Channel Tunnel. Photo credit: English Landscapes.*

made fresh, strong roots that will enable it to withstand a severe gale. Such root development may be encouraged by digging deeply and wide about the new site and ramming the ground firmly after planting. It must be remembered that (except, perhaps, standing in water) nothing is so trying to a moved tree as continual strain upon its unconsolidated roots. The bigger and taller the tree and the more exposed the situation, the greater such strain must be.

Very large, old trees require special apparatus for lifting and moving. Several firms of nurserymen undertake this work, for which they have machinery. If the tree to be moved is a fine and valuable one, this may be done with some certainty of survival if a trench is dug in a semicircle several feet from the stem, by which all roots are severed. The trench should then be filled with good soil, well rammed. The following year a similar trench should be dug

Prunus Aurium Flora Plena *fifteen months after planting.*

A semi-mature tree being moved into position for replanting. Photo credit: English Landscapes.

Adjustable platforms used for cutting high hedges.

on the other side of the tree, roots cut and soil replaced and rammed. Two years later (that is, three years from the first operation) the new fibrous roots which will have been formed will be tough and will stand handling, which they would not stand after one year's growth. Care should be taken to drain the opened ground, that water may not lie in the trenches.

High specimen trees and hedges can generally be reached for clipping from a light ladder resting against them, for by the time the plants have reached such height they have been clipped many seasons and the branches are sufficiently stiff to bear a man's weight on the ladder. Exceptionally high trees and hedges which are very thick require the use of boards resting on painters' trestles. Others may be reached from step-ladders, and there is a form of three-legged ladder used in hop gardens which is very suitable, as one leg can be pushed in amongst the lower branches, so bringing the top close to the work. Generally, it will be found necessary that one person should hold a step-ladder whilst another clips.

LEVENS HALL, CUMBRIA. *Ladders used for access to the top of the topiary for clipping.*

GREAT DIXTER, SUSSEX. *The crow-stepped pediment over the archway, shown fully grown.*

Plate 37. GREAT DIXTER
Semicircular yew archway in hedge, to be surmounted by crow-stepped pediment, now only half formed.

ARCHES AND OPENINGS

There is no more attractive feature in a garden than a vista, and openings in yew hedges present particularly charming effects of this kind. Plate 37 shows a semicircular arch surmounted by a half-grown crow-stepped pediment. The arch was formed by tying together long twigs and shaping with the shears. Where the span is wide or the arch slender, as at Earlshall, Plate 39, a light frame of 1in. x ⅜in.

Well-clipped yews arranged symmetrically along the path leading towards the archway.

Plate 38. SUTTON PLACE. *Yew hedge round sunk pool garden with piers at invervals forming recesses in which tubs of hydrangeas, etc., are set.*

Plate 39. EARLSHALL. *Slender arch of great span, trained on wood battens, which are more unsightly than wire and cord. The piers forming recesses on each side of the path enclose flower plots, for which the competition by roots of yew is too severe. For such positions tubs or boxes of plants are more suitable, as at Sutton Place, Plate 38.*

Plate 40. A LARGE ARCHWAY
A large archway of wide span before training the branches, which for several years had been left to overhang. Note the greater growth on the left side which faces the sun. The wires, quarter inch thick, are fixed to stakes driven into the ground among the foliage. These are connected by tarred cord to which each twig is tied.

Plate 41. THE ARCHWAY SHOWN IN PLATE 37
The archway shown in Plate 40, after the branches have been tied separately with string, and superfluous growths trimmed. The work occupied two men a day and a half.

battens is often set up upon which to train the branches until they are sufficiently stout to support themselves and maintain the shape of the arch. Such an arch takes several years to form, and the wooden framework is very conspicuous; it also occupies too much space and tends to screen the foliage from light. A better method is that illustrated on Plates 40 and 41, where stout stakes were driven into the ground amongst the branches of the yews and to these thick fencing wire, ¼ in. in diameter, securely fixed by winding round the stakes. The wires were then taken across the path and fixed to similar stakes on the other side, forming single-strand wire arches. At short intervals these arches were connected by strong tarred string crossing them. The structure is shown as fixed (before the yew branches were tied up or clipped) and the same structure after each twig had been tied individually to wire or string. The tying was done with tarred string. The arch illustrated was 8 ft. above the path at its highest point, and would allow a fair amount of sunshine to penetrate and

COTTAGE GARDEN, SUSSEX. *This arched and pedimented hedge shields the house from the road whilst still allowing light through its arcading.*

GAMBERAIA, ITALY. *Formal arches pierce the semi-circular hedge round the pond whilst stepped low box shaping emphasizes the curve.*

LEVENS HALL, CUMBRIA. *Twin yews shaped to form a ceremonial arch capped by a crown and flanked by square tapering columns, with ball finials, on domed supports. An extraordinary and celebrated creation.*

HIDCOTE MANOR, GLOUCESTERSHIRE. *Simple arched opening cut to reveal a statue surrounded by wistaria.*

BIDDULPH GRANGE, STAFFORDSHIRE. *Architectural yew hedging shaped to emphasize the Egyptian entrance doorway.*

Plate 42. *Trabeated opening with finials at cottage gate, Horeham Wood.*

encourage growth of verdure. The whole work occupied two men a day and a half and has withstood heavy gales of wind. The growth of the next two years should enable the curve of the arch to be completed accurately. The trees were well manured and the soil round their roots forked up; everything possible was done to encourage growth, especially on the right, where the branches for the arch were required to grow away from the sun. Those on the left, which grew towards the sun, threw out many more and much longer shoots. The trabeated opening over a cottage gate at Horeham Road, Plate 42, is carried out in that ponderous manner which is so well suited to yew and would be still more effective were it flanked by more important hedges. Yew porches and tunnels, Plates 43 and 44, are also suited to the plant, but if these are deep, the light will not penetrate sufficiently within the arch to secure growth of foliage there. The further development of this treatment in the formation of summer-houses is subject to the same limitation within, but the great mass of yew is extremely effective when viewed from without.

Plate 43. *Yew porch at Benenden.*

Plate 44. *Yew tunnel.*

HELMINGHAM HALL, SUFFOLK. *Square-sectioned low box hedges with pyramidical corner finials set out the formal ground plan of a design with an elaborate urn at its centre.*

PENSHURST PLACE, KENT. *Box-edged parterres intended to contain floral planting but here filled with box.*

BOX

The experience gained with yew is also applicable to box, which is really slow growing, but for that reason is especially well suited for positions where miniature hedges or specimens are required. The practice of clipping with a batter is as important as with yew: even for a parterre as that at Penshurst, Plate 45, a slight batter will make all the difference between compact, even growth and lanky, stalky plants. Often the good result derived from batter is marred by the growth of border plants which have been set too close to the box edging or hedge. Some parterres have no

GLAMIS CASTLE, SCOTLAND. *Box hedging emphasizes the formal shapes of the rose beds set out on a level gravel terrace.*

Plate 45. PENSHURST PLACE, KENT. *Box parterre. High yew hedge separates the garden from the path.*

plants growing in the areas surrounded by box, but have the surface of the soil sprinkled with broken sea-shells, or small stones, often of different colours. Such formality, however, is at variance with true gardening, which may better be served by planting the beds with such delicate, slow-growing roses as Comtesse de Cayla. These may be grown alone, without any carpet of violas, which are liable to grow rankly and smother the lower growths of the box. If a carpet is essential, common stonecrop is pleasing and less harmful. In the Box Garden at Earlshall, Plate 46, fancy has run riot in

Plate 46. TOPIARY WORK IN BOX AT EARLSHALL.
Chickens, ducks, baskets, balls, with finials and figures in relief – all in box.

a whole poultry yard of box and in many shaped plants, some of which have initials and other devices formed in relief on huge balls and cones. The whole is carried out in small compass, which should appeal to those who wish to achieve much in little space.

Often old roughly grown box plants may be obtained from old gardens. These will be leggy and all the growth will be on the top. If replanted as edgings and cut to a batter, as described for yew hedges, they will throw out fresh growths from the leggy stems and in three or four

HAM HOUSE, LONDON. *Box hedging, punctuated by cones, contains the planting and enlivens a very horizontal garden plan.*

If box is allowed to get too leggy it may be difficult to prune successfully. Here a new plant has been inserted into a gap, where it will eventually fill the space with the density required.

ANGERS, FRANCE. *Box hedging used to form parterres de broderie and to contain brilliant floral panels.*

Plate 47. VISTA THROUGH ARCHWAY.
Vista through archway, the pediment of which is to be crow-stepped. Note the batter of the well-grown box edging.

years form hedges or edgings 2 ft. high or more, as those seen through the archway, Plate 47, which were treated in this fashion and may be compared with the rectangular edging shown in Plate 48.

By choosing the best plants from such rough stuff, many fancy shapes may be produced quickly. The large cottage loaves planted in the centre of brick piers, Plate 46, were formed in this way, the bunch of taller plants in the middle being tied with tarred string round the waist; shorter plants or plants more deeply buried were set all round and hid the bare stems of the centre bunch. Thus, almost at once large, interesting objects were formed.

Very good box plants, shaped as peacocks, etc., are grown in large numbers in Holland for the English market. After a few months or years they begin to deteriorate and become sorry objects. This usually arises from insufficient

Plate 48. BATEMAN'S.
Vista through yew archway. Square-cut box edging.

Plate 49. COTTAGE LOAVES.
Formed of bunches of old box plants, planted closely (in holes in the brick piers)
and tied with tarred string. They were cut to good shapes in two years.

Tall box plants of rather leggy character provide height whilst thicker box plants fill the lower gap.

Two varieties of box have been used to produce this gold upper finial and deeper green hemispherical base.

A box ball which has become leggy and sparse has here been cut back to produce new growth.

LEVENS HALL, CUMBRIA. *The almost dream-like quality of the shapes developed in this garden have a vivid effect upon the imagination.*

LITTLE HASELEY, OXFORDSHIRE. *A view of the box chess garden, showing the crisp quality of the clipping in producing the chess pieces set out for the 'game'.*

Container-grown box topiary will eventually need larger pots or to be planted out if successful growth is to continue.

room for root growth and from the quantity of soil being inadequate for plants of their sizes. Re-potting (or re-boxing) in larger receptacles, with good soil, will stimulate fresh growth. Where box birds have grown very large, as those in Plate 50, it may be inconvenient to have larger boxes or tubs. In such case the bottoms may be knocked out

LITTLE HASELEY, OXFORDSHIRE. *A view of the chess garden set out before open farmland.*

A GARDEN IN SUSSEX. *This Dutch peacock in box has lived happily in a large tub for six years.*

IFORD MANOR, WILTSHIRE. *An exceptional pyramid of rounded shapes, almost like a jelly mould, capped with a finial.*

ANGLESEY ABBEY, CAMBRIDGESHIRE. *Simple box shapes in urns add formality and calm in flanking a sitting area.*

COMPTON END, HAMPSHIRE. *A creative combination of formal cylindrical and layered shaping capped by a 'bird's' head and fantail to give a strong impression.*

Plate 50. BOX BIRDS.
These box birds outgrew their boxes, from which the bottoms were taken and the roots allowed to go down into well-prepared soil in the ground.

A vista is obtained from the back door by placing tubs of clipped box at intervals down the paving to the pool.

of the boxes, and the soil in them allowed to rest on the ground, which should be prepared by digging a couple of feet down and filling up with manure and good soil. The plants soon root into the earth in such a pit and flourish wonderfully. Boxes as those in the illustration will last over twenty years if made of sound oak. At the end of that time it may be necessary to bore out the oak pins with which they are put together and to build up new boxes of similar design round the cube of earth inside.

Box should be clipped in May or June, when it has made its fresh growth, and again in September, if exceptional growth renders this necessary.

COTTAGE GARDEN. *A whimsical 'house' which echoes the roofs of the real houses beyond.*

RENNES, FRANCE. *Clipping the hedging above a floral display.*

GREAT DIXTER OPENING TIMES
From April to mid-October afternoons only,
closed on Mondays
Telephone: 01797 252878

Plate 51. GREAT DIXTER, SUSSEX.

COLOUR
PHOTOGRAPHS

Plate 52. GREAT DIXTER, SUSSEX. *This plate, circa 1925, shows a yew hedge with uncompleted arch in the front garden. The hedge and arch have since been removed.*

BLACK AND WHITE PHOTOGRAPHS

DRAWINGS

PHOTOGRAPHERS

GERALDINE ANDREWS
2, 3, 7 bottom, 8, 10, 11 both, 16, 18, 20 both, 21, 22 both, 23 top, 26 both, 27, 30 top, 34 both, 37 bottom left, 39 bottom right, 41 top left and right, 42, 47, 49, 51, 52 top, 53 top, 54 left, 56 top right, 57, 58, 59, 60 top and bottom left, 61, 64, 70, 71, 73, 76, 77, 80, 81, 84, 85, 88, 89, 90, 91, 92, 96

ANTIQUE COLLECTORS' CLUB
19, 37 bottom right, 51 bottom, 71, 73, 93

GREAT DIXTER
12, 13, 24, 25, 29, 32, 33, 37, 39 top and bottom left, 40, 43, 44, 45, 46 bottom, 48, 50, 52 bottom, 53 bottom, 54 right, 55, 56 all black and white, 60 bottom right, 61 bottom, 62, 63, 67, 72 bottom, 74, 75, 78, 79, 82, 83, 86, 87, 94, 98, 100, 103

PETER GREENHALF
6 bottom, 7 top, 14, 13, 23 bottom, 30 bottom, 31, 72 top

JERRY HARPUR
Front cover, back cover, 6 top

ENGLISH LANDSCAPES
68, 69

COLIN MORGAN
(CURATOR, NATIONAL PINETUM, BEDGEBURY)
65

Plate 53. WEST BEDFONT. *Yew trees at church gate. The date 1794 is cut in the foliage.*